STRUGGLING WITH
STROKE
Separation From Past Self

DOUGLAS JAMES

Copyright © 2025 by Douglas James.

Library of Congress Control Number: 2016904517
ISBN: 979-8-89465-116-3 (sc)
ISBN: 979-8-89465-117-0 (e)

All rights reserved. No part of this publication may be reproduced, distributed, or transmitted in any form or by any means, including photocopying, recording, or other electronic or mechanical methods, without the prior written permission of the author, except in the case of brief quotations embodied in critical reviews and certain other noncommercial uses permitted by copyright law.

Scripture quotations marked NLT are taken from the Holy Bible, New Living Translation, copyright © 1996, 2004, 2007. Used by permission of HYPERLINK "http://www.tyndale.com/" Tyndale House Publishers, Inc. Carol Stream, Illinois 60188. All rights reserved. HYPERLINK "http://www.newlivingtranslation.com/" \o "NLT Website" Website

Printed in the United States of America.

Integrity Publishing
39343 Harbor Hills Blvd Lady Lake,
FL 32159

www.integrity-publishing.com

CONTENTS

Preface vii
The Event 1
Weariness 7
Emptiness 11
Desire For Isolation 15
Anger 17
Helping Yourself 23
Help From God's Word 32
The Disappointment Hall Of Fame 40
The Disappointment Hall Of Shame 55
The Job Test And Manasseh 62
The End Of Recovery 69
Choice 72
Disconnection 74
Recap 77
Final Thought 82

Dedicated to Marcella

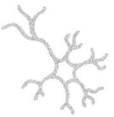

PREFACE

This book is about my stroke in my sixty-second year, which was bad enough to incapacitate me physically for several months. I experienced none of the effects associated with severe strokes: my cognitive ability was intact; my memory untouched; very little was wrong with my facial muscles, and therefore, eating and talking were minimally affected. Consequently, this book is not meant for severe stroke victims who struggle with the tragic loss of cognitive ability, memory, and/or communication ability. Similarly, this book is not meant for severe stroke victims who are tragically truly incapacitated physically with very little hope for improvement. Even though I had a bad stroke, I cannot imagine the difficulty and heartbreaking experience of a truly severe one. I don't presume to have anything of import to say to these individuals. I do not share their experience and cannot speak of it. Comments here concerning improvement methods are certainly not directed at them.

My stroke left me in the following condition. During the ten days I was in the hospital, I could not stand up from a seated position without help from hospital personnel, and I could not walk without both a walker and support from hospital personnel. Just sitting upright in a padded chair for an hour was too difficult. Standing without holding on to something was too difficult. Getting into a seated position on the edge of my bed on my own power was barely possible. These effects were tough to deal with, but others less tangible were much worse. It is this other group that is the primary focus of this book, effects such as severe anxiety/ restlessness, physical and emotional weariness, emptiness inside or a disconnection in the soul or an unfamiliar self- presence, the desire for isolation, and anger.

The fact that my stroke was not extreme left me completely conscious during the entire experience. I was fully aware of the progression of all the stroke's effects. Consequently, as time passed, I learned from conversations with other stroke victims, and especially their caretakers, that I possessed a perspective that may be of some value for others with strokes of similar severity to at least make some sense of their own experience, or hopefully help them cope a little easier, or perhaps even help with recovery progress.

A stroke is a devastating thing. It feels exactly like brain/ muscle connections and nerves have been burned or fried. In addition, this also happens to a person's psyche or soul. In the long sleepless nights in the hospital and nursing home, I could find no peace and very little rest. I felt adrift, alone in a vacuum or in a desert. Anxiety went beyond worrying about the logistics of being able to care for myself or finances; it was a living companion that continually writhed inside. I felt like a big part of my soul had been burned from being too close to a fire or spraying acid. A lifetime of experience in communing with the Lord was simply gone, with no ability to pick up where I left off— that is, before the stroke. Basically, a stroke means inability to move on the outside and restless disoriented emptiness on the inside. In addition, your body aches, especially your head and neck, your hips and core muscles. Your body is always wanting to simply slump into a chair with your head fallen to your chest, your left side slightly curled up, your eyes closed, and your mind blank. Trying to keep your head up is a weariness. Your core muscles are so weak that they have trouble exerting enough force to blow your nose effectively.

THE EVENT

For several years prior to my stroke, I experienced a variety of minor neurological discomforts. Auras in my vision would occur several times a year, increasingly accompanied with mild to severe dizziness. I would mention these in my annual doctor visits, but they were ignored. During treatment for my stroke, I learned that at least some of these instances, certainly the last one about six months before my stroke, were TIAs (transient ischemic attacks) with severe spinning dizziness and some nausea. Three months prior to my stroke, I suddenly was stricken with Bell's palsy and, for about two months, was unable to move the muscles on the left side of my face. I could barely eat, and talking was difficult. However, the effects of Bell's palsy completely cleared up within two months. The doctors assured me that my stroke was a recent development and had no connection at all with these prior experiences, even the TIA and the Bell's palsy. But I never accepted this diagnosis, primarily because on the morning of my stroke, during the drive to church, I experienced auras and dizziness, exactly like those experienced previously.

During the service, these gradually cleared up, such that I started the drive home feeling normal. But as the drive progressed, I again felt slightly dizzy, along with something new: a general disconnection with the environment. Staying in my lane required more-than-normal conscious effort. So I stopped for a burger, thinking my head would clear up if I took a break. It seemed to be working until I was halfway through the burger. A sort of wave flowed across my brain, and suddenly, I could barely chew and swallow. I couldn't manage to tear open the plastic ketchup containers for my fries, so I just bundled up what was left of my meal and dropped it in the trash. I had to lean against the wall for a moment or two to get my balance before heading to the parking lot. The last ten miles to my house were difficult. Staying in my lane was even harder than before, and it felt like I would never get home.

I have a tight interior spiral staircase up to the second floor, and about halfway up, my left leg collapsed underneath me. The staircase is like a cage, so I didn't fall anywhere. For the first time, I felt scared as I pulled myself up the last few steps to the kitchen floor. Once on level ground, I grabbed the railing and was able to stand up. I was able to walk around slowly, and so I immediately started doing step-ups on an eight-inch-high step I had used to install a light fixture. I kept doing step-ups with both legs until my left leg was working as good as my right. During these step-ups, I picked up a three-pound ankle weight in my left hand and was exercising my left arm, which was not wanting to work either. After about fifteen minutes, I felt better and lay down on the couch and picked up a book and read for a while. I felt fine and made a call to the nurse in our family, telling her that I had just had a stroke and that I would go see a doctor first thing in the morning to get checked out. She made me promise that if I had another episode, I would immediately call 911 and go to the emergency room. This was about 2:00 p.m. About 5:30 p.m., I was sitting on the couch, working on my laptop, and suddenly realized that I couldn't move my left arm at all. I had not felt anything happening to me while I had been sitting there, but when I tried to stand up, I immediately crashed to the floor because of absolutely no strength in my left side. I couldn't get up, so I crawled behind the couch to pull myself up and promptly crashed again. There then ensued about twenty or thirty minutes of trying to walk around the house and continually falling down until I finally admitted to myself that this time I wasn't going to be able to shake it off. So I managed to get into the bedroom and lay down, after only two more falls, first into the hall wall and then into the foot of the bed. After two seconds of lying in bed on my back, my first experience with anxiety occurred, and I simply could not stay still but had to struggle into a seated position on the edge of the bed and start kicking my left leg around and moving my left arm around in scrunched-up little circles. Everything felt really bad at this juncture, and I had to come to grips with going to the ER. I reasoned that since I couldn't walk without falling, there was no point in waiting for the morning since I couldn't make it to the car anyway, much less drive.

Somehow, while on the phone with 911, I walked out of the bedroom, down the hall, across the living room, over to the sliding glass doors that opened on my deck, and unlocked the doors so that the paramedics would be able to get in. I don't know how I managed to do all that without falling again, but I did, and then I sat down on a futon bed by the doors and waited for them to show up, with the 911 operator still on the line encouraging me. Her comments were extremely helpful. The trip to the hospital was about an hour drive, and it was a relief for two reasons: (1) it's always calming to talk to professionals when you really need them, and (2) it was a great relief to discover that I had no problem with speech or communication and that I was not having any mental lapses or cognitive problems.

A night and a day in ER were not that bad because they kept me sedated pretty heavily, and the official news, after several tests, that I had had a stroke was certainly nothing new—from the moment I felt different while eating my burger, I knew precisely what was happening to me. Although it was very difficult, I managed to send text messages to family and friends while in the ER to let them know I was mentally okay—I just couldn't move and felt terrible, but not to worry about cognitive problems.

The move out of the ER into my own room in the same hospital was a welcome change because it made me feel more like a patient with a possible future, as opposed to just an uncertain emergency case. When asked about my pain level, I gave a moderate rating, since pain seemed irrelevant compared with being paralyzed on one side of my body. However, as the days progressed, I was glad that I had indicated that I did indeed have a significant pain level because the doctors prescribed doses of morphine. Although my pain was real and grew worse in the first few days, and needed sedation, my main problem was severe anxiety/restlessness. Each passing day reiterated that a live anxiety companion had taken up residence in my soul in a big way. If I had not been prescribed the morphine, I would not have been able to lie still or rest at all. It is very hard to describe, but the anxiety was just as much of a physical thing as it was an emotional one. My body simply would not be at rest unless sedated. If you have ever experienced "restless legs," just multiply that by a factor of about five or higher and call it "restless body."

This anxiety continued through my ten days in the hospital, my three weeks in the nursing home, and also after I returned home, especially at night. However, I gradually began to sleep longer periods, and eventually, the anxiety left me. Fortunately, this most difficult effect of the stroke was temporary.

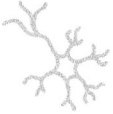

WEARINESS

The first week in the nursing home was basically horrible for two reasons. One, the anxiety continued unabated, but now there was no morphine available. Prescribed pain medication was only ibuprofen, and anything given for anxiety seemed to have no effect at all, neither did sleeping pills. Therefore, by 4:00 or 5:00 a.m. each sleepless night, I was reduced to a half-naked blob sitting in my wheelchair and slumped over the narrow table with wheels that was used to hold my food tray. Staying in bed all night was just not possible. I broke the house rules by climbing into my wheelchair without help and moved around in little circles to be in motion. I liked things on wheels because I could jerk them back and forth a little and get the illusion of a little comfort. Fortunately, I only crashed to the floor one time, getting back into bed after one of these unsupervised nocturnal excursions around my little world. I was assisted back in bed, of course, after I had crawled to the call button, but I was on their watch list from then on. Somehow I generally managed to get an hour or so of sleep before breakfast at seven thirty. I think it was more of passing out than falling asleep.

The personnel at the nursing home were great, regardless of their area of employment or expertise. They were all my first friends in my new post-stroke life (more about the life-separation issue later). The only time I had a little difficulty with the personnel was on my first day, and it wasn't their fault. There was a policy that the heads of the various departments needed to contact all new patients as soon as possible to learn their particular needs in order to plan and maximize the benefit of their stay. Since I was doing nothing at all on my first day, except lying in bed and waiting for meals, it was an excellent time for them all to come by my room. It was a good policy, and I learned a lot from all the visitors; however, it was also my first serious experience with weariness. After each visit, I would collapse back on the bed, completely exhausted from yet another conversation about my experiences of the prior ten days. Whenever you happen to be around a stroke victim and are tempted to think that they could surely sit up a little straighter or be a little more active or at least be more alert, especially in conversation, please consider that weariness from a stroke, especially a recent one, is like a big monkey on your back continually pushing your head and neck down on your chest with one hand and grabbing your left wrist with the other hand and twisting your left arm into a ball on your chest and yammering in your ears the whole time. The only time there is relief from this feeling is when you are lying flat on your back in bed undisturbed.

To illustrate the tenacity of weariness, about three months after my stroke, when I had made considerable progress in physical therapy, such that I was living on my own and walking with a cane, I was waiting in the drive-through at McDonald's. Weariness was on me pretty bad that morning, and I was slumping down in the driver's seat to rest while waiting for the cars in front of me to file through the drive-through. I must have looked a lot worse than I thought because the lady in the car in front of me had paid for my breakfast when I got to the window. She must have noticed me in her rearview mirror. And this was on a Monday morning on my way to my therapy session after a weekend of better-than-average rest.

Physical and emotional weariness go hand in hand. A stroke victim seldom, if ever, wants to get dragged into a lengthy conversation. Excess questioning may foster anger and resentment. Criticism may foster rage. Control of emotions, in general, is very much affected, such that outbursts of anger and weeping can occur in chronological proximity with equal magnitude.

Since physical and emotional weariness becomes a major problem in the stroke victim's life, one is forced to embrace the horrible word "management." Since weariness will obviously persist as a big part of one's life for a long time to come, one has no choice but to attempt to manage it.

Personally, I've learned not to wait until the weariness has overcome me before I rest. Generally, I try to get some rest mid-afternoon, about twelve hours from the midpoint of the nightly sleep. Studies show this is the most effective time, whether sleeping or just idle. If being around certain people wears me out, I avoid those people like the plague. If certain activities frustrate me unnecessarily, that is, if an unpleasant task can be eliminated, I eliminate it. If the weariness demands that I take more time alone to process events and recharge, then I don't make any plans and become ruthless about unwelcome interruptions. Bottom line, you have to set your own boundaries and parameters and defend them vigorously if you expect to manage the serious problem of weariness.

EMPTINESS

There is a correlation between physical effects and those in the immaterial world. A stroke attacks the nerves that carry messages from the brain to the body's muscles. But it goes far beyond just a roadblock in the process. The brain does not know where all your body is. In physical therapy, the first thing one learns is that your affected limbs feel exactly like they are floating alone in space somewhere, disconnected from your body. Consequently, it is obvious and easy for the patient to understand the phrase "the pathways from brain to muscles must be rebuilt." "Tell me something I don't know," they all immediately think.

My standard physical therapy regiment of a few months has long been completed, yet every time I stand up, I have to pause for several long moments before I start to walk in order to give my brain a chance to "feel my legs." While I'm pausing, I involuntarily sway slightly, front to back and side to side, while my brain is getting its bearings. When walking, the same thing occurs, with a chronic drifting to the left with every step. Before a stroke, your brain is very aware of your body, such that you can go from a rest position immediately into walking or running or jumping. After a stroke, if you try to immediately start walking as soon as you stand up, you will do a face plant nearly every time. This is much more apparent at night when getting up for a midnight snack or for a restroom break. The body tends to solidify when lying motionless, and walking around at night feels like you have regressed toward the helpless days in the hospital. You learn to keep some lights on so you can see places to grab onto, even though it has been months since you needed a cane.

These physical disconnects have a direct correlation with your inner life. In the same way that your brain needs to relearn where your body is, your psyche or soul needs to relearn self-awareness as well. I can't say what needs to be restored. I can only describe the experiences I have had. I doubt if anyone, besides the Lord God, has any definitive idea of the invisible intricate pathways that need to be restored. He is the only one who understands them when they are perfectly healthy, much less when damaged. How can immaterial functioning be directly affected by flawed physical biology? Again, only the Lord knows. We are intricately made—our body and soul are most certainly intricately connected, not at all separated or isolated from each other.

There is an emptiness inside caused by a stroke that I describe as a vacuum or a desert place. I meditated during the long nightly hours on the simple question, "What happened to me?" or, much more accurately, "Where did I go? And will I ever come back?" and "Who is this new guy sitting on this bed? He's different. I don't know him."

Gradually, I became familiar with "the new guy" as I realized I must embrace him as me and forget about recreating the "old guy." The old guy is never coming back; he's dead and gone. There is a wall of shadow between you and your old life that will not dissipate. In my case, everything back there was still intact—memories, how I felt about everyone I remember, goals, dreams, etc. But it was separate, it was over, it was a gray world with no color photographs. All that happened to someone else. Many of those things will get pulled into your new life and take on similar emphasis; also, many will not. The point is that you are now a different person, and you have no choice but to embrace it and go forward with the new you.

The best analogy I have come up with to help me with this is what I call the California plan. I once read a fascinating article about the boom years in California in the gold rush days. Hundreds of thousands of people who had utterly failed in the Eastern United States at jobs, relationships, or whatever, rushed off to California to "reinvent" themselves. California in that period was perfect for doing that. Everyone over there in the boom years had gone belly up at least once, maybe numerous times, but were currently embracing yet another California plan with equal enthusiasm. This was possible simply because there was zero stigma upon failing in the culture there. Fail back in the East and stay there and you may never raise your head again. Fail in California and no one even bothers to ask what you had been trying to do. It was like the culture was always saying, "Failed?" Of course, I've failed. Been there, done that, bought the T-shirt, I have a closet full of them. But here, take this free brochure about what I'm doing now. It's dynamite.

DESIRE FOR ISOLATION

We all have different innate levels of preferred social interaction according to our different temperaments. However, I believe it is safe to say that all stroke victims look forward to being completely alone, certainly in the initial stages, primarily to try to rest to prepare for the next interruption, which is sure to arrive in a matter of minutes. One thing that is as certain as the sun coming up is that another tiring ordeal has you in its sights and is closing in on you as you lie there in your bed or rest in an easy chair: a nurse with medication, a nurse checking your vitals, personnel bringing meals, personnel coming to take you to physical therapy or occupational therapy or a meeting about your progress and estimated release date. Even family and friend visitations, though certainly welcome, will drain you badly.

Back home, these occurrences are replaced with task schedules, and the same thing continues. Everyday tasks like showering, dressing, cooking, answering the phone, cleaning up, shopping, etc. become the tiring ordeals that leave you wanting to lie down and have as long a period as possible that you do absolutely nothing and deal with absolutely nobody.

Another aspect that encourages isolation is embarrassment. No one wants to be seen moving around so slowly and awkwardly, or continually dropping things in the kitchen, or having trouble responding promptly to questions. And then there are worse things: falling in the presence of family and friends and the occasional close calls of barely making it to the facilities in time because of severely weakened core muscles.

Strokes make conspicuous spectacles of people, and it is natural for stroke victims to seek to be alone as much as possible. The difficult part for family and friends is that this aspect of a stroke tends to be permanent. One's desire for social interaction lessens going forward, some more severe than others, but it is an effect that is shared by all victims.

ANGER

The last effect of a stroke to be discussed is anger. It is the last effect to manifest itself, and it is, by far, the most difficult one. In fact, each of the effects discussed so far occurs in the same chronological order as they appear here. First comes severe anxiety and restlessness, then comes great weariness, then there is a frightening huge void in connection and self-awareness, then a determined position of isolation is adopted, and finally anger sets in. Of course, all the effects continue together and gradually reduce at different rates, so several are generally always with you.

Anger generally occurs when one has entered into recovery, having moved forward from what I call the trauma period. In fact, anger is actually a healthy sign that one has entered into recovery mode. Anxiety has dissipated sufficiently to not really be a big problem anymore; sleeping has even approached normalcy. Weariness is still there and will continue to be there for a long time, but one has begun to learn to manage it, and weariness does gradually reduce in proportion to the level of exercise and therapy performed.

The disconnection in the soul has not diminished at all, but it is such a mysterious aspect that one simply accepts the new state of being—that is, there literally is nothing one can do about it, other than just wait for the new life to become the norm, which happens on its own. In fact, conscious efforts to help this process actually make it worse. This is God's territory; you must simply wait on him and trust in him that he will make you as whole again as is possible in light of what has happened to you.

However, with anger, we enter into a different world. This one is the killer. Unlike the other effects, this one has much more potential to change one's outlook and personality for good. Certain people may not have as much of a problem with it as others. For some, anger may simply be connected with the frustration of physically performing tasks. However, it is very likely that this will not be the case because the vast majority of stroke victims are not young. Young people are always focused on the task at hand, the current goal in sight, the achievement just around the corner. Their energy level and youthful drive enable them to make a stroke event into more of a big unwelcome skid mark on their road of life, rather than let it become a life-debilitating event. In general, it is tough to keep a young person down, compared with those of us who have lived the majority of our lives, who have fought all the struggles, and who have become accustomed to reaping the rewards of our labor. It is not so much that we are worn out or worn down by life. It is more like we have finished the race and graduated successfully, and now, in the midst of our reward, we are cut off at the knees and get thrown back to the starting line. This is not an easy situation to be in even if finances are not a problem, even if living independently is not a problem.

The tough part about anger caused by a stroke is that it is multifaceted and progressive. Initially, anger occurs just from the difficulty of moving around and performing tasks. This stage of anger is not directed at anyone. It is simply aggravation, frustration, inconvenience, and embarrassment. However, soon one directs anger at oneself, when these things continue unabated for a long time, with only slow progress gained toward competence. Obviously, you can't get away from yourself. It can be a very debilitating habit to be angry at yourself in a permanent way because of a lessened state of competence at basically everything. This is a much more serious problem than many realize. One of my therapists helped me with this in an unexpected way. I was doing occupational therapy, which, for me, at that time was performing intricate tasks with my left hand: picking up tiny objects off the table and dropping them into a box. I was frustrated and gave my left hand a slap and said something like, "This stupid thing just won't work." She looked at me with such seriousness and deep concern that I was taken aback. She simply implored me, "Please, please, never talk like that about your own hand. It's part of you. You aren't stupid."

Everyone is on a different point on the continuum of forgiving yourself. I happen to be very hard on myself, even to the point of replaying mental movies of all my failures or embarrassing moments. I don't let myself off the hook easily. Incompetence from my stroke caused a lot of self- blame. Even though I knew it wasn't my fault that I had a stroke, in my mind, it was my fault that I still couldn't do things with my left arm and hand, walk normally, interact normally, deal with life normally, etc. Anger at yourself for incompetence can literally stay with you for the rest of your life.

The final stage of anger may not happen to most people. This is when anger tends to shift from anger at oneself to anger at God. Ironically, those who love the Lord the most are the most at risk of this last aspect of the anger problem. The reason is obvious. They have grown to love the Lord so much in their lives because he has done things for them in the past for a long time in a very personal and deeply appreciated way. They have become accustomed to be continually aware of him and are deeply connected with him. These people are totally blindsided by the effects of a stroke that affect one's ability to have connection with the environment, with their own soul, and with the Lord.

For these people, anger at God is not what you would expect. It is not anger that he allowed the stroke to happen to them or even (in their worst moments) that he did it to them on purpose. Although these thoughts and feelings will certainly occur, they do not generally persist. No, it is much different from that. They are stymied by the fact that they cannot connect with him because the stroke simply strips them of this physical/spiritual ability. They have been unable to feel his comforting presence at all during the worst experience of their lives. They quite understandably think that God has abandoned them, that he has refused to give them even a few moments of peace, that he has refused to come to their aid. They don't even feel like the same person anymore and begin to doubt whether their spiritual experiences in the past are even applicable anymore or valid; that is exactly as if those experiences happened to someone else. It is true that they have not had any peace or any comfort or any connection. But what they don't realize is that the reason for this is their brain and soul have been fried enough to block their ability to sense him, not that he isn't there or isn't concerned.

Over time, a hopelessness and resentment can set in with people in this category, of which I was one. As diminishing returns begin to occur in the area of physical therapy, this hopelessness can grow proportionately. As one approaches the level of physical competence, which will be the new norm going forward, it is similarly difficult to continue to improve in the areas of emotional outlook and energy in one's soul. Extra effort in pulling your emotions up by the bootstraps— which, at first, was actually reasonably easy because of the many encouraging people around you— becomes more and more difficult. Your outlook emotionally begins to match the reduced expectations for physical progress. The body and soul are intricately connected, as discussed previously, and move in tandem, like a yoke of oxen, for better or worse, for good or bad.

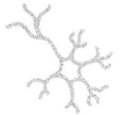

HELPING YOURSELF

The somewhat cursory comments in the prior sections concerning improving your situation during each of the effects of a stroke were generally descriptive and not intended as a definitive self-help aid. Those comments, however, are certainly worthy of some embellishment in that direction.

One must engage in a progression of opposing a stroke's effects. In a general sense, this attitude is really quite natural. It is much more natural for people to try to get better than to give up entirely and get worse from doing nothing. It is hard for us to understand why someone just stops trying in any area of life. It is easy for us to understand when people pause for a period from discouragement to regroup or examine their options, but giving up entirely is actually foreign to human nature. It is never an admired decision. It is human nature to keep trying. When toddlers fall down on the carpet, they continually and immediately get back up and keep going without any parental encouragement. This behavioral attribute holds true for our whole lives.

In revisiting the effects of a stroke, the main point is to establish the one key winning response to each effect. No doubt there will be many pauses in opposing a stroke's debilitating effects, and no one will fault a stroke victim for taking their due rest periods or short-term sabbaticals. Hospitals and nursing homes are certainly sensitive to this, and although daily therapy sessions are scheduled, these are kept to strict time limits to avoid overtaxing the patient. Once back home, it is important to continue at the same pace, to continue "doing the work," but to continue also to get your rest. Very likely, this will take a friend or family member to encourage and help with set times to duplicate the therapy exercises learned, at least at first. It is very important not to focus on the level of progress but rather simply upon doing the sessions. These have now become your new full-time job.

For combatting anxiety/restlessness, the key response is not an easy one. The only cure is time because, although this is a very difficult effect, it is temporary. One must simply adopt endurance as the only effective response. Anything external (primarily medication and social interaction) that can lessen this effect is obviously to be encouraged, but only endurance will get you through to the other side. Eventually and gradually, peace and rest and normal sleep patterns will return. Continually making yourself consciously aware of the truth—that this will soon pass—keeps these difficult days in perspective.

Weariness also is somewhat temporary in that it steadily improves, although it will never be totally gone. For this reason, the best response is always managing one's activities. A full day of activity is best followed with a more restful day with nothing much on the schedule. The weariness from a stroke is like a background condition. It is not like sore muscles from too much exertion; it is much deeper. It resides more in the ligaments and bones than in the muscles; at least that's how it feels. Time is one's best ally, along with acceptance of new limitations and patience.

Tiredness and weariness are very different, at least for a stroke victim. Tiredness is a healthy good feeling that follows physical exercise or extended activity. It makes one want to kick back on the couch with feet up, a glass of iced tea in one hand, the remote in the other, and heave a sigh of relief. Weariness is sitting down looking at the nearest horizontal surface longingly, wanting to lie down on it, and then lie still and just wait to die.

Strange as it seems, the best short-term cure for weariness is getting tired. For a stroke victim, weariness is a condition, a companion; it is a chronic sore stiff aching neck and a slight nagging headache, along with other aches. It is worst when sitting in an uncomfortable chair. I never sit at a kitchen or dining room table unless I absolutely have to. It just feels terrible. But when one is in motion, in a therapy session for example, weariness is much less noticeable. Doing the exercises substitutes healthy tiredness for debilitating weariness. It is more than just getting your mind off it; it is a true substitution. Feeling tired from exercise makes you feel like a normal person again. You will likely get that iced tea and grab the remote and surf channels or call a friend. The more you substitute tiredness for weariness, the better you will feel and the more normal you will feel. But it isn't easy. You have to force yourself to get into motion *while* you are feeling weary. Before your stroke, you had to fight laziness in order to exercise. That was tough enough, but fighting off weariness to get in motion is harder. Although it is counterintuitive to expect exercise to dispel weariness, it does exactly that. Each person must find personal triggers to help them get into motion, perhaps rewards afterward or the satisfaction of achieving a higher level in the exercises. For me, nothing at all worked, except telling myself very firmly that it was simply the right thing to do.

Emptiness is a mysterious effect, and there's not much to be added to the prior comments on this topic. As stated previously, the key to combatting this effect is associated with adopting the correct attitude of acceptance. Your old self is gone and will not return; your new self is here to stay. No effort should be expended in recovering anything. Think of it as an adventure, learning life again, and trust God to keep buried what needs to be buried but also to make new things. As far as positive activity is concerned, it is important to adopt what I call the Building the Forms Method. You are responsible to build the wooden forms and trust the Lord to pour in the cement to make new things. For example, is there emptiness in communing with the Lord? Then decide to attend church regularly, *as if nothing is wrong*, and expect the Lord to pour in the reality of the experience. Approach devotions exactly the way you approach therapy sessions; simply do the work, do the right thing, *as if nothing is wrong*. To build the empty wooden forms, simply do the right things and wait on God to fill them. Do friends just not have the same fulfillment they once did? Well, go ahead and sit down with them anyway, *as if nothing is wrong*, and try to let good things start to happen to you. Remember, no one, not even the Lord, can build the forms for you. If you don't have a few forms built and ready to receive, the flow of cement will never begin—ever.

Alcoholics Anonymous has a street version of the Building the Forms Method. It's called Fake It till You Make It, which is exactly the same thing. Their core principle is to rely entirely on God (officially "higher power") to make the crucial internal changes as they remain faithful to keep the external behaviors. The ones who succeed are the ones who accept down to their bones that they cannot do it themselves and that if they do not succeed, they will certainly die, sooner rather than later. You will never hear a successful member publicly or privately say that they made it on their own strength. They never forget the secret to their success—zero trust in themselves. That's why they stand up in meetings, no matter how many years of total abstinence they have achieved, and begin by saying "I am an alcoholic." They are not degrading themselves or humbly ignoring admirable successes. They are telling the truth. They are simply maintaining the crucial bone-deep knowledge that they *always* need help, that they are *never* strong enough on their own.

Christians (the real ones) have also deeply learned this same knowledge. They stand up every Sunday, regardless of how many years they have dedicated themselves to faithfully following biblical principles, and begin by saying "I am a sinner." They are not degrading themselves or trying to appear humble. They are telling the truth. They know that they cannot do it by themselves and that if they don't succeed in internalizing God's strength, they will certainly die spiritually, sooner rather than later. They are simply maintaining their core principle that they *always* need God to fill them internally as they remain faithful to keep the external behaviors. You will never hear a real Christian publicly or privately say that they made it on their own strength. They never forget the secret to their success—zero trust in themselves.

The desire for isolation can be a real problem, even a permanent one. However, if the effective positions are adopted in the other areas, isolation will not likely have a sufficient opportunity to entrench itself. More so than in any other area, the persistent attention of family and friends in the face of avoidance on the part of the patient is the strongest positive, as long as it is done in a low-key manner. Never let it be in any way a big event with lots of people in a party atmosphere. This approach will fail miserably and most certainly push the patient further into isolation. Short one-on-one visits, or with two at most, is the way to handle giving ongoing attention—in other words, exactly how you would approach a normal friend on a normal uneventful day. Don't initiate any stroke topic at all—everyday boring, even mundane, topics is the way to success in bringing patients back toward the same level of social activity they exhibited before. The huge need of a stroke victim is to feel as normal as possible; we want to blend in to the scenery as flawlessly as we can. The very last thing we want is to hold lengthy discussions about ourselves or any lengthy discussions at all. I'm still looking forward to being able to go into public places and not be noticed as someone who is having difficulties.

As mentioned previously, the real enemy is anger. There is no cure for anger other than good old-fashioned self-control. Unfortunately, later on in the process, if anger continues beyond simple frustration into self-blame, one must attach mental assistance to the self-control in order for it to be strong enough to work. A time will come when telling yourself that things could certainly have been much worse will not get the job done. You won't care about that anymore once you have been in recovery territory long enough and have been unable to make much progress. This is simply human nature. Knowing and telling yourself the truth that you have much to be grateful for will not keep calming you down. You will need something stronger to defeat your enemy.

Ultimately, you must actually observe and/or come in contact with people who *are* worse off than you are. Fortunately, this experience is always strong enough. It is powerful and immediately effective to restore a grateful humble heart. We shouldn't need this strongest of medicines; being grateful for the level of independence we have gained since the stroke event should always be enough. We should easily be continually cognizant of how helpless we once were and how far we have come. But we do need it because it is human nature to forget the past, feel sorry for yourself, and seethe in self-pity and anger. It is human nature to forget where you were and only focus on where you want to be, where you should be, where you deserve to be after all you have suffered and continue to suffer but that you just cannot attain. When all this starts to overwhelm you, when you become jealous of every person you see who can walk normally, step effortlessly over speed bumps, and be active physically, when your anger cannot seem to be assuaged, it is crucial for you to tell yourself that you are not evil or wicked; you are simply human. We are not perfect human beings. We are all, every one of us, fallen human beings who gravitate to base behavior when diligence in guarding our hearts becomes weakened with suffering.

HELP FROM GOD'S WORD

Unfortunately, helping yourself, no matter how effective, will not be enough. Of course, it won't. But we have the wealth of God's word to join in harmony with our own efforts. If one's ability to effectively hear from the Lord personally (communion) becomes weak or absent, it is of no real consequence. The written word is more than adequate to meet our needs. It abounds with examples of people who faced severe disappointment. In the portrayal of their lives, it provides the correct responses that make a way through. The following are a sampling of this great treasure of help.

THERE WAS A KING

Everyone knows who *the king* was—fearless in battle, intense in faith, never-wavering in loyalty, the standard for all of us to emulate. Everyone loves his poems, songs, hymns, and praise. But when it comes time for us to get a grip on severe disappointment in life, David seldom comes to mind as a poster boy. Everyone knows his victories, his triumphs, his great standing with God and man. But few focus on his trials without cause, his forced isolation, his undeserved branding as national enemy number one, his life as a hunted animal in deserted places far from God and people, his lengthy time of denial in receiving the promises of God spoken to him personally, his life of forced friendship with outlaws and criminals, the most desperate of men.

The Bible, of course, makes no effort to hide or dilute these difficulties of David. They are all clearly presented with no ambiguity in the books of history. But they tend to pass quickly through the reader's mind, and one's attention is soon enthralled with the hero enjoying his due place in the historical narrative, firmly established as king with all enemies silenced.

However, that is not how David himself discussed his own life. Although his psalms are obviously upbeat and foremost in unmitigated praise and worship to the Lord, there is also an abundance of his personal despair and deep disappointment within these same psalms. There was a long list of hardships throughout his life, none of which defeated him.

David was despised in his own immediate family. He grew up as the youngest in a large family in an atmosphere of being the one who was ignored, looked down on, considered to be of no account, the one to be ridiculed by all. Yet David developed no resentment toward his family; he did not suffer from a poor self-image. He boldly grasped the first opportunity for personal recognition, despite the scorn of his elder brothers and the doubts of the king, and slew Goliath.

David was quickly and permanently hated by the king for his selfless victories in battle, simply because they were greater than the king's. The king personally tried to kill him and kept hunting David down like a dog for the rest of his reign. David became a forced exile, condemned by the king's decree. He was cut down and cast out while his well-deserved fame was in its infancy. The promise of God given personally by the prophet became effectively null and void. Yet David matured as a man without once giving in to resentment or retaliation. He held his integrity intact during the worst of times, and he endured.

Immediately after David's great enemy was taken out of the way, he had no respite from persecution. Instead of being welcomed back into the good graces of the nation, his political enemies fought a seven-year civil war against him to deny him the kingship. He was outnumbered with just one tribe in twelve loyal to him. Yet again, David persisted, and slowly, his fortunes improved, and his goal was achieved. There is no record of David ever treating the other enemy tribes as second-class citizens during his subsequent reign. There was no vengeance.

Then after David became the undisputed king, one of his favorite sons began a systematic usurping of the throne. For four years, Absalom worked tirelessly against his father, stealing the loyalty of the nation. Absalom came within a hairsbreadth of supplanting his father. Yet David ordered no retaliation; he harbored no ill will toward his son.

The cries of David's heart through all these hardships and disappointments are recorded for us within the same psalms of praise that are loved by all. His responses, given to us in complete openness and honesty, document the correct way to handle both the anger from severe long-term disappointment, as well as all the other effects discussed above: anxiety, weariness, emptiness, and isolation.

Consider David's words, right off the bat in Psalm 3:1–2: *O Lord, I have so many enemies; so many are against me. So many are saying, "God will never rescue him!"*

This can be taken as the topic sentence for all David's personal words throughout the 150 psalms. He, at once, talks as if he and the Lord are one in his trials. We immediately learn that David has publicly declared his faith, in no uncertain terms, that God was able and willing to give him victories over his enemies because that is their favorite deriding taunt: "his God is unable to help him." David calls this out to the Lord, equating his own enemies with God's enemies. This tells us of David's integrity. He doesn't think that he brought his enemies upon himself by his own shortcomings. He knows they are without cause and that they are primarily directed, not at himself, but right in the face of God. David is not being arrogant and vindictive; he is being boldly humble, speaking from a pure heart toward God. Our own walk with the Lord seldom allows us this certainty—that is, that our difficulties come from consistently living for God's causes. As such, we struggle with boldly asking the Lord for action like that stated a few verses further on in Psalm 3:7: *Arise, O Lord! Rescue me, my God! Slap all my enemies in the face! Shatter the teeth of the wicked!*

David seldom, if ever, prays like modern Christians. By this, I mean, praying carefully to "take all aspects into consideration," like the possibility that we might be in the wrong and deserve it or like the possibility that the enemies were wrongly treated by others earlier and were driven to their actions effectively involuntarily. No, David just asks God to smash them in the face so hard that all their teeth are not just broken but also completely shattered. Isn't that disturbingly harsh and unchristian? Could David have used a few New Testament directives like love your enemies or judge not? Perhaps. Were things that different in his age, so much more clear cut and easily understood at face value? Perhaps. However, the real question to ask is this: Is David's character the subject of this text, or is David's love for God's causes on display here? There are indeed sections of scripture where David's character flaws are brutally portrayed for all future generations to clearly see with no ambiguity whatsoever. However, the Psalms are not among those sections. Passages such as these in the Psalms give us the cries of the heart of David, the man after God's own heart, during his actual times of severe persecution and hardship. We desperately need to know these heart responses; we desperately need to know exactly how he felt and what he said about it to his God in prayer. Other than the inner workings of the heart and prayers of David, the king, we have only the heart responses of the Lord Jesus himself in the gospels. But many of David's prayers undeniably give us the very heart responses of Jesus. The Psalms are like the Holy of Holies in the scriptures. I believe we must maintain this viewpoint in order to get the help we need, the help God intends us to gain, from the cries of *the king*.

Psalm 5:1–3: *O Lord, hear me as I pray; pay attention to my groaning. Listen to my cry for help, my King and my God, for I pray to no one but you. Listen to my voice in the morning, Lord. Each morning I bring my requests to you and wait expectantly.* Long-term anxiety is clearly reflected in this passage. Morning after morning, the same request is made. David's soul is groaning for relief from a continual condition of anxiety. Psalm 5:7 provides the answer for his condition:

Because of your unfailing love, I can enter your house; I will worship at your temple with deepest awe. As is so often the case in the Psalms, understanding and relief come from entering the presence of the Lord.

Psalm 6:2–3: *Have compassion on me, Lord, for I am weak. Heal me, Lord, for my bones are in agony. I am sick at heart. How long, O Lord, until you restore me?* This passage certainly fits the many days that stroke victims spend in anxiety and weariness as deep as their bones.

Psalm 6:6, 9: *I am worn out from sobbing. All night I flood my bed with weeping, drenching it with my tears . . . The Lord has heard my plea; the Lord will answer my prayer.* Often in the Psalms, a verse appears like this last one. Two things have happened in the believer's heart. First, there is a certainty that God has heard the prayer. This is like a judge agreeing to hear a case in court and having placed it on the docket. Second, the believer rests in the knowledge that the Lord will decide in favor of the believer. The first is past tense. The second is future tense. The first shows a connection has been reached after dedicated prayer, perhaps over many days or years. The believer has successfully entered into the Lord's presence. The battle has been won at this point. Waiting for the favorable outcome will take care of itself; it is being looked after by the Lord himself in the court of heaven. These two separate statements are together saying the exact thing that was said in Psalm 3 about entering and worshipping in God's temple. It is the same event, the same answer.

In Psalm 7:3–5, we find David qualifying his prayers for deliverance. *"O LORD my God, if I have done this and there is guilt on my hands—if I have done evil to him who is at peace with me or without cause have robbed my foe—then let my enemy pursue and overtake me; let him trample my life to the ground and make me sleep in the dust."*

At first glance, this appears to refute the earlier comment that David rarely prayed as modern Christians do—that is, doubting themselves. But the severity of his self-proclaimed punishment shows again that the king is concerned about adherence to God's principles, rather than concern for his own safety, so much so that he far prefers his own complete destruction to compromise in God's laws. We don't feel that way. We add comments about our own possible guilt much the same way we tack on to the end of prayers a mechanical "according to your will Lord, not mine," or "in Jesus's name."

Space prohibits covering all the other numerous instances of the heart cries of *the king*. They appear throughout the book of Psalms. Thank God there was a king. Thank God he struggled as we do. Thank God he shared his mind, heart, and soul with us. Thank God he showed us the way.

THE DISAPPOINTMENT HALL OF FAME

This is a book about extremes. A stroke brings a plethora of extremes. It seems fitting in this section to focus on the most extreme biblical examples involving the handling of deep disappointment.

JOB: The Best There Was

Any discussion of experiencing hardship and disappointment simply must begin with Job. He was literally the textbook legal case. The Bible declares in Job 1:8 that Job was God's best man on the planet in his lifetime. *"Have you noticed my servant Job? He is the finest man in all the earth. He is blameless—a man of complete integrity. He fears God and stays away from evil."* It could very well be true that Job still holds the all-time title even after thousands of years.

Everyone knows that Job lost all he had: his children, his assets, and his health. But it goes on. His wife is no comfort to him, which is understandable since she had lost everything as well and loved the children as much as Job, probably more, not to mention her complete loss of security. But his friends, although sympathetic, unexpectedly proved to be no comfort either. In fact, they continually accused Job of bringing his troubles and grief upon himself because of his hidden sins, which, obviously, in their minds must have greatly proliferated, given the punishment laid upon him. They bring new meaning to the phrase "kicking a man when he is down." Then in the final ordeal, the Lord himself shows up and subjects Job to a lengthy legal interrogation, almost as if he agrees with Job's friends. Of course, Job is unable to answer any of the Lord's questions.

However, as everyone knows, the story has a happy ending, with Job's friends rebuked for their false accusations and Job's fortunes restored at double what they were.

Job is the classic case of someone who had it worse than we ever did. It's a good idea for a stroke victim to make the book of Job required personal reading.

NOAH: The Only Man

Noah is included here for what is probably an unexpected reason for most readers. Noah did not lose anything personally in his role as the effective savior of the human race. But during the 120 years* that he labored on the ark, he also preached to the population, imploring them to repent of their wickedness and be saved. No doubt he hoped that God would change his mind if enough people repented. However, like the prophet Jeremiah, he convinced no one at all. He endured the constant ridicule of his neighbors but worse; Noah certainly experienced great sorrow watching and hearing all the people drown. The Bible says that the Lord himself closed the door of the ark before the flood began. He knew that Noah would probably have opened it to let the people who were screaming and beating desperately on the door in. It is very doubtful that Noah looked out from the ark gloating on their plight. It seems certain that he shared the Lord's feeling, as given in Ezekiel 18:32: *For I take no pleasure in the death of anyone, declares the Sovereign LORD. Repent and live!* It was not a pleasant experience, after a 120-year grace period, for Noah to still be the only man who pleased the Lord and to be chosen to perpetuate the human

---

* To help bring this into a very realistic time frame, Noah built the ark in 120 years, probably with only the help of his three sons and with no modern equipment. This is about four or five times as long as it took the Harland and Wolff Company in Belfast, Ireland, to build the *Titanic*. However, they used fifteen thousand workers and modern equipment. The ark was half as long as the *Titanic* (450 feet versus 859 feet). The *Titanic*'s capacity was for three thousand passengers. The ark was designed to hold a great deal of livestock, rather than passengers. It took two years to float the *Titanic*'s hull (fifteen hours on weekdays and ten hours on Saturdays). The hull was finished in just four months in dry dock, but it took seven years to build the dry dock (none was large enough). The ship's interior was finished in four years. All this excludes years of design work. Both ships were used one time, one successfully (Belfast Titanic Society).

race. For the rest of his life, he lived in an empty world with empty stone cities half buried in mud as constant reminders of the huge loss of life. In many ways, Noah truly lived out one of our favorite science fiction themes as one of very few survivors of a lost civilization, dwelling among gradually collapsing structures.

Sadness was certainly a big part of Noah's life, to a level beyond anything any of us have experienced. Meditating on his story may help lessen sadness and especially emptiness in the heart of a stroke victim. Noah lived in an empty world. Literally everything he did was building new things.

ABRAHAM: The Founder of Faith

Abraham is famous for believing God's promises during many years that the fulfillment of those promises was simply impossible according to the basic and inescapable facts of human existence. In other words, Abraham was the first to depend solely on miracles to receive what God had personally promised him. Believing for a miracle as your only hope in life is extremely trying in any age, ours included. But Abraham held his faith firm in the face of impossibility for many years. But it was worse than that. Beyond hope, the promises of God were actually fulfilled! However, this reality was enjoyed for only a relatively short while. Suddenly, Abraham was commanded to kill his son, the fulfillment of the promises.

The biblical account of the journey to the stipulated place of execution reads like a slow-motion movie. Abraham's actions are mechanical but obedient. It can only be surmised that during this journey of several days out into the wilderness, the father of faith reasoned out the only answer—God would have to bring his son back to life from the dead in order for the promises not to be broken. Obviously, the Lord could have chosen to do that and let Abraham go ahead and do the deed. But as we all know, he stopped Abraham once he saw that he was really going to do it, stopped him a split second before the point of no return.

Many lessons can be learned from Father Abraham, but for our purposes here, the main point is that Abraham, in deep disappointment, continued for a long time that the promises of God had not been fulfilled and finally were impossible to be fulfilled, and yet he continued to believe.

Any stroke victim could certainly use a miracle or two, however small. Every time I find myself able to do something new in my physical repertoire, even if it's just more feeling in my left toes, it feels like a miracle. When a dead part of me comes to life and starts to respond, what else can it be called? Abraham's story is encouraging and gives us hope. He received miracles.

JOSEPH: The Beloved of His Father

Joseph, the favorite son of Jacob, experienced one of the most difficult lives in the Bible. He was persecuted for many years by those whom he had not wronged. Joseph is one of the few biblical characters who did not have any recorded shortcomings. He was blameless. At seventeen, he was sold into slavery by his own brothers because they hated him for being favored by their father. As a slave in Egypt, he was wrongfully accused by his master's wife and thrown into prison. After helping a fellow inmate gain his freedom, the man failed to speak on Joseph's behalf, as he had promised, and Joseph remained forgotten in prison. Thirteen years passed since he had been taken from home, and he was without hope, without friends, without family, and living in prison in a foreign land.

Finally, the Lord executed his master plan for Joseph's release, and in one day's time, Joseph became the ruler of Egypt, answerable only to the pharaoh himself. Up until that morning in his thirtieth year, Joseph had no inkling of what the Lord had planned to do to save two nations, Egypt and Israel, from a severe famine. Thirteen years of severe disappointment and hardship is a long time, especially for a young man, but Joseph held on to his integrity and his faith in God and was ultimately rewarded.

Joseph's story is one of remarkable endurance, a crucial weapon needed in stroke recovery. Joseph was aware of God's attention in his circumstances during his hardships. He was elevated to favored status in the house of his master and also with the head jailor. In other words, although he was not dwelling in comfort or freedom or in God's presence, he recognized God's presence behind the scenes, and it gave him strength to endure. A stroke victim may not be in comfort or freedom or be able to feel God's presence, but a conscious effort must be expended in order to recognize God's orchestration of circumstances for them for good in the midst of hardships. It will give strength to endure to better times.

MOSES: The Broken Man

Similar to the life of David, few people would pick Moses as a prime example of experiencing disappointment. Everyone is very familiar with his early success and high standing in Egypt (even if only the Hollywood version) and especially his huge success later upon his return to Egypt to perform the miracles of the Exodus. It is easy to skip over the few verses that fall between these two impressive periods. And it is even easier to miss the huge change that occurred in Moses himself between these periods. In Egypt, whether or not he vied for the throne against a true son of the pharaoh, Moses was a mighty man. In Acts 7:21–22, his Egyptian status is declared in Stephen's sermon at his execution: *Pharaoh's daughter took him and brought him up as her own son. Moses was educated in all the wisdom of the Egyptians and was powerful in speech and action.* Compare this with the description of Moses at the burning bush after no less than forty years of living as a nobody, herding sheep in the desert far from any significant human activity.

> **Exodus 3:11:** *Moses said to God, "Who am I, that I should go to Pharaoh and bring the Israelites out of Egypt?"*
>
> **Exodus 4:1:** *Moses answered, "What if they do not believe me or listen to me and say, 'The LORD did not appear to you'?"*
>
> **Exodus 4:3:** *Moses threw it on the ground and it became a snake, and he ran from it.*
>
> **Exodus 4:10:** *Moses said to the LORD, "O Lord, I have never been eloquent, neither in the past nor since you have spoken to your servant. I am slow of speech and tongue."*
>
> **Exodus 4:13:** *Moses said, "O Lord, please send someone else to do it."*

Moses is now a totally broken man. He apparently does not even remember that he used to be a powerful speaker in his past, much less a powerful man of action. Josephus, the well-known first-century Jewish historian, wrote of the traditions of Moses from the sources of antiquity available to him in his day. He wrote of Moses as a great general of Egypt who led a successful invasion of Ethiopia by approaching unexpectedly through impassable snake- infested swamps. He brought flocks of ibises with his army that attacked the snakes and made a clear passage. At the burning bush, he ran from a snake. At the burning bush, he begged for God to just leave him alone in his misery and go away.

In his youth in Egypt, Moses was aware of his Jewish background.

> **Exodus 2:11:** *One day, after Moses had grown up, he went out to where his own people were and watched them at their hard labor. He saw an Egyptian beating a Hebrew, one of his own people.*

Given his privileged position of authority and his highly developed skill set, he had correctly reasoned that he was supposed to be the great deliverer of his people. Unfortunately, in his first foray into achieving this role, he succeeded only in ruining any chance he had to fulfill his calling. For the next forty years, he had plenty of time to meditate on what could have been, what should have been, what he was supposed to have. Forty years is a very long period of deep disappointment, especially when you brought it on yourself by foolish impulsive behavior.

My stroke was caused by blood clots hitting my brain. Others are caused by internal bleeding in the brain. But the underlying cause is seldom certain. My doctors were unable to tell me what had really caused my stroke to occur. I rarely used alcohol or tobacco, exercised regularly, never had a sweet tooth, and generally avoided red meat. The only things I could isolate as possible contributing factors was a high-blood-pressure condition (controlled with medication for ten years prior to the stroke) and a tendency for cholesterol levels to be somewhat above the normal range. Therefore, I had no alternative but to accept the fact that, over the years, I had not been careful enough with medication and/or my diet was worse than I thought. It has been a constant painful regret in my mind that I must have brought my stroke upon myself from lack of diligence in these areas over time. However, Moses had this same constant painful awareness a lot worse than any of us for a long period of forty years. But God had mercy on Moses and gave him a second chance. Anyone who survives a stroke and achieves independent living has also been given a second chance.

DANIEL – The Flawless Servant

Beloved Daniel is another man like Joseph with no recorded shortcomings. He too was blameless. He too was taken prisoner to a foreign land about the same age as Joseph. Although Daniel was not placed in a prison, he was not really free, and he faced execution twice in Babylon before he achieved honor from the king. Like Joseph, he rose to an influential position but with a total of no less than three great kings: Nebuchadnezzar II of Babylon, Darius the Mede, and Cyrus II of Persia. Like Joseph, Daniel never returned to his home, but unlike Joseph, he never was blessed with a family. It is likely that he was castrated as a young man when he was ordered to take his place as a member of the magician class in Babylon.

Daniel lived a life of involuntary service to foreign rulers and never, as we say today, "had a life." Even when he was living in the courts of foreign kings, he was not a free man, more of a privileged specialized slave. Despite this, he was renowned for his piety and faithfulness to God. God honored Daniel before these kings, and his influence was not wasted on the three great monarchs he served. It is clear from the account of Nebuchadnezzar that this great king became a saved man, no doubt because of Daniel's flawless witness. Cyrus the Great is highly spoken of in scripture as being God's chosen servant. Both Darius and Cyrus were very kind to the Hebrews and allowed them to return to their land, again, no doubt because of Daniel's pristine visible example of a life dedicated to God.

It is very easy for a stroke victim to feel like he or she no longer "has a life." Even if independent living is regained with communication and cognitive abilities intact, as with me, it's still very easy to feel that way. Daniel's fine example, someone who really didn't have a life, is worthy of reverent meditation on our part for inspiration in this area.

PAUL: The Chief of Sinners

The life of Paul the apostle stands alone in terms of hardships suffered for the cause of Christ. The words of the Lord to Ananias who was sent to receive Paul after his conversion define what Paul's ministry was going to be like: **Acts 9:16:** *I will show him how much he must suffer for my name.*

Paul single-handedly founded the Gentile church. He rarely had a period of peace as he relentlessly, selflessly, and successfully followed his calling over many years. Paul never faltered in his ministry. No New Testament person can stand with him in terms of difficulties encountered and had overcome in ministry. Yet Paul's own description of himself is the title of this section. Of course, he is referring to his zealous persecution of Christians prior to his conversion. No one knows the internal torment he bore because of this unfortunate period in his early life. No doubt it was acute and extensive, no doubt often overwhelming.

However, none of this addresses disappointment, which is our topic here. There is a somewhat hidden strain in the scriptures concerning Paul that needs to be pieced together from scattered verses. He had more than deep regret and remorse to deal with during his life. He also experienced deep disappointment, and unlike the previous people discussed, this disappointment was *never* reversed with fulfillment.

Paul, by his own admission, was a Hebrew of Hebrews, trained in the top school with the top teachers. Today we would call him the "golden boy" of the ruling Pharisees. He was foremost in learning, foremost in zeal, foremost in skill. He was the chosen instrument to travel and bring the "Christian heretics" back to justice. He knew his future among the ruling circles in the ruling city of Jerusalem was secure. No position would be out of his reach in his future career. In addition, it is clear from biblical accounts that Paul had the arrogance to match his credentials. Throughout his life as an apostle, the Lord had to "keep him humble" by means of the mysterious thorn in the flesh, most likely difficulty in his sight.

Paul deeply yearned for the recognition a high position in the Jerusalem church would bring. He knew he was more than qualified. He knew he understood the scriptures better. He knew he had done more. He knew his road had been harder. Yet his entire ministry was conducted far away from the center of his world, the seat of prestige and power. He was never allowed to be part of the "in crowd," the "inner circle."

No, instead of fulfilling his destiny in Jewish circles, Paul spent his life in lowly, dusty, Gentile shacks and strange foreign locations, making tents and teaching in homes rather than churches, many times in towns where people barely knew where Jerusalem was or what it represented. There was never any prestige, there was never any recognition, there was never any of the professional respect he knew he deserved. In the rare instances when he traveled to Jerusalem and met with the "genuine" apostles, he felt compelled to point out their failings, as with Peter and his posturing with eating Gentile food. There is one small instance of recognition by a Jerusalem apostle, Peter, the same man whom Paul corrected in front of everyone, given in **2 Peter 3:15–16:** *Just as our dear brother Paul also wrote you with the wisdom that God gave him. He writes the same way in all his letters, speaking in them of these matters. His letters contain some things that are hard to understand, which ignorant and unstable people distort, as they do the other Scriptures, to their own destruction.*

There is no indication that the Lord ever lifted the sentence of the thorn in Paul's flesh, and no indication that the Lord ever allowed Paul to stay in Jerusalem long enough for a firm connection to be established with the other apostles. Sometimes God's answer is no, and it stays no.

Strokes usually occur during the retirement years, when there is finally the time, the opportunity, and hopefully the money to pursue a dream or two as a personal capstone to one's life. Unfortunately, a stroke will probably wreak havoc with such a plan and perhaps negate it permanently. If this happens, and the answer stays no, well, the apostle Paul knew exactly how you feel, to an extent far beyond your understanding. You are in excellent company. The greatest man of the church age was told a resounding "No" over and over his whole life. Those who fall in this number do well to read and study his letters, to do their best to enter into his understanding. "No" may end up being the best thing that ever happened to you.

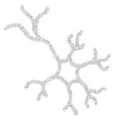

THE DISAPPOINTMENT HALL OF SHAME

Perhaps the most revealing aspect in this dubious group that represents the other side of the disappointment coin is the small level of disappointment that occurred in the lives of the two worst ones: Cain and Judas. Esau also fell in this category. These three were barely offended. The following examples represent disappointment pitfalls that, God forbid, any of us could fall into if diligence in guarding our hearts erodes.

CAIN: The Devil's Own

Cain is famous as the world's first murderer. He killed his brother Abel because of jealousy. Jealousy that was carefully and lovingly addressed by the Lord God himself in a personal conversation with Cain, in which Cain was assured that he could obtain favor also if he brought a correct offering—that is, one with shed blood. It is unclear if Cain had simply not understood or if Cain had rebelled or, more likely, if Cain simply placed no significance on the offering and was just going through the motions. Although the Bible does not state that God had commanded the men to bring offerings, it appears that this was the case. The issue was that, unlike Abel, Cain did not approach the Lord on the Lord's terms. Of course, the whole incident also reveals the condition of the two men's hearts, which was the underlying issue. Abel understood and loved the ways of God, and Cain did not. But Cain resented missing out anyway, so much so that he killed because of it.

Cain was a very evil man. The Lord's conversation apparently had no effect, except that of, "So you want blood? I will give you blood." Even when Cain was shown mercy, he immediately rebelled against God's judgment. Instead of accepting his sentence as a wanderer, he defied the Lord and built the world's first city. Since the ground would not produce food for him, he had to become the first middle man and live off others' produce through commerce moved through his city.

ESAU: The Man of Flesh

Esau also was smitten with jealousy, pure and simple. In his case, it was more pathetic because he had already agreed to give away his birthright. Upon reflection, however, Esau regretted the decision and was jealous of Jacob receiving what he had freely given him.

Esau simply had no mind or appreciation for the spiritual things of God, and he continued in this mind-set his whole life. Like Cain, he simply was not capable of doing anything, except going through the motions, when it came to anything pertaining to God. He was like Saul, the first king of Israel, who just couldn't catch on to why a sacrifice would not get the job done on its own.

The church today is well-represented with people like Esau and Saul. They participate in baptisms, offerings, ceremonies, and prayers while missing out on the spiritual reality and then become mystified and angry and jealous when the physical benefits do not readily flow into their lives. They assume that Christianity is just a formula or two. Just do it and get it over with and you are in.

JONAH: The Despairing Prophet

Little is told us about the life of Jonah. He is one of those characters whose sole appearance covers only the most disparaging event in his life. Jonah obviously had a successful ministry with the Lord in his past because he had learned over time that the Lord rarely, if ever, punishes anybody. Unfortunately, this was Jonah's problem with God. God was way too nice. Jonah had yearned for a fire- and-brimstone judgment to accompany all the outings that the Lord had sent him on. But he never got any. God always pardoned them all. Finally, this enraged Jonah so much that when he was commanded to go preach to Nineveh, he refused to go. Nineveh was the horrendous bloodthirsty capital city of the Assyrians. Their brutal practices earned the title for Nineveh of the "City of Blood." In other words, this last mission for Jonah was to go to the worst place possible and tell them to repent; people deserving to burn so badly it was ridiculous. Assyrians would routinely cut open the stomachs of captured pregnant women, throw the fetuses in the air, and spear them just for the entertainment value. Jonah didn't go because he already knew what would happen. God would pardon them, and nothing would be done. Once again, no punishment. Jonah couldn't take it anymore. As it turned out, Jonah was exactly right—God did end up pardoning Nineveh.

Jonah certainly appears to have had a unique disappointment problem among the prophets. However, it does speak to us because we all question God too at some point. Part of the anger that stroke victims experience is sometimes directed at God personally. This is no different from what Jonah did, finding fault with God for both things he has done and for things he has not done. No matter what our problem with the Lord is, we simply have to get off that bus as soon as possible because we are wrong about him. Even if he goes ahead and once again does what we are mad about, we are still wrong about him. There is never anything wrong with the Lord. The Bible doesn't tell us if Jonah ever came around and repented of his anger at the Lord. But the implication for us is clear. We just can't ever go there; it will do damage to our souls for no good reason whatsoever. And this kind of damage, which is caused by anger, can be permanent, a real soul killer.

AHITHOPHEL: The Wronged Official

Ahithophel was King David's chief councilor. He had the amazing reputation of never being wrong. It was said that his words were as if the Lord himself was speaking. Ahithophel's son, Eliam, was one of David's thirty mighty men, and Eliam had a daughter, Bathsheba (Ahithophel's granddaughter). Bathsheba was the wife of Uriah, the Hittite who was also one of David's thirty mighty men. Ahithophel joined in Absalom's rebellion against David because David had inflicted serious harm to Ahithophel's family and honor. David had made Bathsheba pregnant and then murdered her husband Uriah by ordering him to be placed in the most dangerous parts of the battlefield. So David committed adultery with Ahithophel's granddaughter, then killed her husband, and then took her to be his wife.

Ahithophel obviously learned of all the details of these events from Bathsheba herself over ensuing years, as well as from his son Eliam. For many years, Ahithophel lived with the bitterness of this deep disappointment and loss (the dishonor to his granddaughter and also the death of Uriah, who was a very honorable man). Late in David's reign, when Absalom plotted to kill David, Ahithophel became Absalom's councilor and saw that the day of his revenge had come. His advice to Absalom was perfect, as always, and would have defeated David. But the Lord caused Absalom to follow other advice and thwarted his coup attempt. When Ahithophel saw that his advice would not be followed and that David would not be defeated, he committed suicide.

Such serious harm to a man's direct family cannot be borne without miraculous help from the Lord. Even more difficult for Ahithophel was the fact that he was working face-to-face with David in his inner circle for years after these events as his chief councilor, fully knowledgeable of what David had done. This disappointment is perhaps the most painful and difficult of all biblical examples. Unfortunately, it proved more than Ahithophel could bear, and he made the wrong decision.

JUDAS ISCARIOT: The Devil's Own

Everyone knows who betrayed Jesus to the chief priests and Pharisees, but not everyone knows the primary reason that Judas Iscariot did this deed. Judas had a problem with the love of power and money. He managed to be placed as the treasurer of the disciples so that he could easily steal from the offerings given to Jesus's ministry. However, this love of riches went beyond just wanting some petty cash. The disciples were all expecting Jesus to overthrow the Roman government. They were thrilled with this coming event as patriots and lovers of God and his people. Although this was a misguided hope, it was a common belief of what the Messiah would do when he came. However, Judas's motivation was simply to cash in on the wealth and success that the eventual rebellion would surely bring to those who were Jesus's closest companions. Having witnessed the miracles of Jesus, it was not hard to expect Jesus to perform this feat. However, as Jesus's ministry showed less and less promise of achieving this aim, Judas felt more and more disappointed and betrayed. He so deeply wanted power and money that he was convinced that Jesus should die for deceiving him and wasting over three years of his life. Of course, Jesus never told the disciples that he was going to overthrow the Romans, but in Judas's mind, that just added to the transgression.

The truly sorrowful part of Judas's end was that he actually loved Jesus to a certain extent. This was evident from the deep remorse he experienced after he had betrayed the Lord. Unfortunately, he could not bring himself to approach God in prayer, receive forgiveness, rejoin the disciples, and become one of the dynamic characters of the book of Acts. He took the route of Ahithophel and committed suicide.

THE JOB TEST AND MANASSEH

This chapter seemed appropriate for the sake of completeness, if nothing else. There is little doubt that any stroke victim will eventually fail, to some extent or other, mentally or verbally, what I call the Job Test. There is a disturbing section of scripture that at the height of Job's suffering, his wife urges him to "curse God and die," in effect "stop holding out for no reason and just commit suicide." However, despite this "encouragement," Job did not sin with his mouth; he passed the test.

I don't know if the Lord used to kill people out of hand for cursing him to his face back in Job's day. I don't know what exactly a curse of that nature would entail. What I do know is that, in our time, the Lord will not kill you if you become consumed with anger, such that you get bitter and harbor resentment toward him. I know this to be true because I am not dead. During the initial trauma period, I did not have this problem. However, difficulties during the recovery period would tend to overwhelm me at times, and

I'm sure I thought of, and even verbalized, imagined divine slights sufficiently to qualify as failing the Job Test.

There is a different kind of guilt that descends on a person when he is harboring resentment toward the Lord. It is a heavier, more serious type of dark blanket with a past-the-point-of-no-return fear associated with it. We find ourselves thinking that our attitude may prevent us from seeking the Lord again in communion as we used to. This is especially true if we get stuck in the resentment mode for a significant time. A recovery phase from a stroke is not really a short period and is powerful in causing and keeping a victim in a bitter mind-set.

Fortunately, despite what you may have thought or said in your worst moments, there is no limit to God's mercy. It is true, on the other hand, that when it comes to God's patience, there is definitely a limit. Eventually, he is going to discipline you and me. If you are his child, sooner or later, he will say "Enough" and move into correction mode. Similarly, it is true that there is also a limit to God's wrath. In fact, his wrath is generally rare and short-lived despite what you may think from Old Testament events. But when it comes to God's mercy, it is literally without end. And the Bible provides a section of scripture as proof, a case study in mercy, if you will.

Manasseh was blessed with perhaps the Godliest of all parents, King Hezekiah and Queen Hephzibah, yet he was, by far, the worst king of Judah and is identified as being the primary cause of the destruction of Israel. An illogical train of events persists in the Bible concerning fathers and sons. The best fathers tend to have the worst sons, and the worst fathers tend to have the best sons. Consider the following father-son pairings as evidence.

First, the good kings of Judah and their bad sons. It's hard to find better men than these kings of Judah, yet they all produced bad sons. (1) David and Absalom: Absalom tried to take his father's kingdom and would have killed him if he had succeeded. (2) Solomon and Rehoboam: Rehoboam is famous for permanently dividing Israel with his very first speech as king and also for performing idol worship. (3) Jehoshaphat and Jehoram: Jehoram was the eldest, and Jehoshaphat made him king five years before he died, but as soon as Jehoshaphat was dead, Jehoram killed all his brothers, anyway, to be sure he would remain king. (4) Jotham and Ahaz: Ahaz was arguably the second worst king of Judah, next to Manasseh, because of instituting many abominable false worship practices, including sacrificing at least one of his sons to idols. (5) Josiah and all his sons: Josiah rivaled David as the best king of Judah. The Bible states that Josiah's godliness and reforms almost caused the Lord to repent of his planned desolation of Israel because of Manasseh, yet the reigns of his sons hastened and ensured this destruction.

Consider Samuel and all his sons as another prime example. Samuel fulfilled the dual role of prophet and judge of Israel. He was the later counterpart of Moses; these two men were like bookends of the period of the judges. Yet Samuel's sons were like false priests. The whole population of Israel begged Samuel to give them a king as his successor and not any of his sons. A further classic example is Jacob and all his sons (except Joseph and Benjamin). His sons sold their father's favorite son into slavery.

Second, consider these bad fathers and their good sons. (1) Jesse and David: Jesse treated David as barely one of the family. (2) Eli and Samuel: Eli was a poor judge of Israel and a weak priest. His sons desecrated the offerings and committed fornication with the women who brought them. (3) Saul and Jonathan: Saul continually sought to murder Jonathan's best friend, David, and was furious with Jonathan for being David's truest supporter. (4) Ahaz and Hezekiah: the actions of Ahaz were mirrored by his grandson Manasseh. Hezekiah likely witnessed one of his brothers sacrificed in idol worship by his father, Ahaz.

However, an astounding development is recorded in the later years of Manasseh's life. He was in prison in Assyria with no hope of escape. In his misery and his bonds, he called out to the Lord for mercy. And the Lord both heard his prayers and answered him. Manasseh, unbelievably, was restored to his kingdom late in life. Manasseh's evil deeds had spanned many decades.

This is the main section of scripture that describes Manasseh's deeds.

> **2 Kings 21:2–16:** *He did what was evil in the Lord's sight, following the detestable practices of the pagan nations that the Lord had driven from the land ahead of the Israelites. He rebuilt the pagan shrines his father, Hezekiah, had destroyed. He constructed altars for Baal and set up an Asherah pole, just as King Ahab of Israel had done. He also bowed before all the powers of the heavens and worshiped them. He built pagan altars in the Temple of the Lord, the place where the Lord had said, "My name will remain in Jerusalem forever." He built these altars for all the powers of the heavens in both courtyards of the Lord's Temple. Manasseh also sacrificed his own son in the fire. He practiced sorcery and divination, and he consulted with mediums and psychics. He did much that was evil in the Lord's sight, arousing his anger. Manasseh even made a carved image of Asherah and set it up in the Temple, the very place where the Lord had told David and his son Solomon: "My name will be honored forever in this Temple and in Jerusalem—the city I have chosen from among all the tribes of Israel. If the Israelites will be careful to obey my commands—all the laws myservant Moses*

gave them—I will not send them into exile from this land that I gave their ancestors." But the people refused to listen, and Manasseh led them to do even more evil than the pagan nations that the Lord had destroyed when the people of Israel entered the land. Then the Lord said through his servants the prophets: "King Manasseh of Judah has done many detestable things. He is even more wicked than the Amorites, who lived in this land before Israel. He has caused the people of Judah to sin with his idols. So this is what the Lord, the God of Israel, says: I will bring such disaster on Jerusalem and Judah that the ears of those who hear about it will tingle with horror. I will judge Jerusalem by the same standard I used for Samaria and the same measure I used for the family of Ahab. I will wipe away the people of Jerusalem as one wipes a dish and turns it upside down. Then I will reject even the remnant of my own people who are left, and I will hand them over as plunder for their enemies. For they have done great evil in my sight and have angered me ever since their ancestors came out of Egypt." Manasseh also murdered many innocent people until Jerusalem was filled from one end to the other with innocent blood. This was in addition to the sin that he caused the people of Judah to commit, leading them to do evil in the Lord's sight.

Any sinful thoughts or words any stroke victim may have committed against the Lord in their frustration and pain, although needing due repentance, cannot begin to compete with the evil life of Manasseh. And Manasseh was not only forgiven but was also restored in response to his repentance in prison. The mercy of God is without limit.

Of greater importance to us in this age is that the real pitfall of anger during a difficult time, such as a recovery period from a stroke, is not that we become angry at times and lose control, but that if you are not careful, this behavior can evolve into a set belief or condition of not trusting the Lord with your life anymore. Of course, that has always been the ongoing battle we face in this life—that is, to continue to trust him. In good times, we must never fall into the pit of forgetting about God just because we find ourselves in abundance and are convinced nothing can shake us. In bad times, we must never fall into the pit of resenting God just because we finally really desperately need him but can't seem to find any blessing. The simplest admonitions from the book of Proverbs are the most profound: "Guard your heart." "Hide the Word of God in your heart." "Meditate on his statutes." It is not easy for us to read Psalm 119 and stay interested in the text because it just keeps repeating the same principle over and over. But we need to hear it over and over until we think it over and over and until we say it over and over. If we can just successfully internalize these admonitions, they can save our souls from self-destruction.

THE END OF RECOVERY

Perhaps the best indication that one has completed the bulk of the recovery period is the same indicator that showed that one had entered it. Instead of anger commencing, anger starts to dissipate. Daily tasks are finally performed sufficiently well that you find yourself thinking about other things while you are dressing, cooking, eating, walking, etc. The level of concentration required to perform tasks has approached normalcy, such that as you get yourself up and around, you are thinking of what you need to get done that day, rather than being completely engrossed in the mundane tasks that have caused so much frustration and weariness.

Another indication is being surprised by involuntarily starting an action that up until now, you never tried but suddenly feel that it would "come naturally." An example would be starting down a staircase facing downward, instead of turning and backing down the stairs facing up as you have been doing. At times like this, no doubt you will stop yourself in time because of the constant vigilance for safety that has become second nature. However, strongly consider "going for it" instead. Your mind and body are telling you that a connection has been restored, and it needs to be established by repetition. Do it carefully, but go for it.

Still another indication is that the scary weird feelings of not remembering what "made you tick" in your prior life (that old guy) become quite isolated. You still don't ever feel like the same person, and you still wonder where you went, but the fear and loss feelings that accompany this phenomenon only hit you in isolated instances, and they become more and more fleeting and less and less powerful, sort of like a freak strike of lightning on a barely rainy day.

In my case, an indication that I was nearing the end of recovery was the return of the desire to reach out a little to others. I have never been one to initiate social interaction, and probably never will, but introverts have the same desires for sociability as extroverts do. They just can't act on them as readily. It's like they are always driving with the emergency brake on. Noticing that I was feeling like it would be a good thing to go visit so and so was a welcome indication that the grip of desiring isolation was loosening somewhat.

It is very important to understand that the "end of recovery" does *not* refer to regaining physical prowess approaching pre-stroke levels. That really has nothing to do with it. Unfortunately, that is the only definition that your family and friends will ever carry around in their minds.

When they heard the therapists at the hospital use the phrase "total recovery," they didn't realize that it was at least half propaganda for the benefit of loved ones. Of course, it doesn't do the patients any harm, they immediately know it for what it is, and they don't believe it for a minute.

End of recovery means that you can now perform all necessary tasks for independent living, albeit more slowly and less gracefully, *without getting angry*; that you seldom are *immobilized* by disturbing vacant self-awareness issues; that you do not *succumb* to slumping down in the middle of the day from weariness; that you do not *refrain* from social interaction because of feelings of either inadequacy or weariness or desire for isolation. It is very unlikely that a stroke victim will ever completely regain the prior level of physical ability. It is unlikely that weariness, accompanied with constant bodily aches, will completely dissipate. A stroke victim will always feel an emptiness at some level. It is doubtful that the same level of social interaction will return. Some personality changes will be permanent. But full recovery *can* be achieved, as long as you understand the correct definition.

CHOICE

The final word to discuss is another horrible word like "management." That word is "choice." In the ultimate analysis, human beings really only have one power, and that is the power of choice. "Choose this day whom you will serve," shouted Moses to the nation of Israel at the holy mountain. "Choose life," says the Lord.

The huge problem we all tend to have about choice is that we all think it means one time. Choose one time and you are good to go from then on. Nothing could be further from the truth. Choosing correctly is more than a once-a-day action, much less a one-time action. Choosing correctly is necessary each and every time your heart and mind start to wander down the pitfall pathways. It is exactly like steering a car. When do you straighten out the car as you go down the road? When do you carefully edge the wheel left or right to stay on the straight and narrow lane of success? The answer is obvious—*every single time* the car has begun to wander off. No one points the car where it needs to go and then stops steering from then on. And you can't wait for a few wanderings to occur and then correct several of them at once, not if you want to stay alive.

Since any stroke victim, by definition, is basically already in a stressed or frustrated condition at any given time, his or her personal "car" starts to wander much more quickly and much more radically than a normal person's. It's not fair, but all aspects of life now require an increased level of vigilance in guarding your heart, which simply means an increased frequency of choosing correctly. It is not easy, but that is our mission that we must continually choose to accept. The only alternative is giving up completely, which is the path to nowhere, the path to oblivion.

DISCONNECTION

We must revisit the issue of the soul floating somewhere in vacant space. In the revised definition of full recovery, this effect of a stroke was said to be sufficiently handled if one has ceased to become *immobilized* in their daily behavior. And this is an accurate definition. However, achieving an active daily life, albeit at a reduced level, is not the whole story. When a person is busy doing something, planning something, thinking specifically about something, talking with people, or just being in the presence of other people; these activities keep one distracted from the background reality of living in a vacuum inside yourself. In times of idleness during the day, or especially when waking up from sleep either in the morning or during the night, disconnection in the soul can hit a person quite hard. As time goes on, these instances become less of an emotional anxiety event and more and more of a reaffirmation of a state of disconnected existence. There can be the entrance of suicidal thoughts because of the tenacity of the effect of your soul being fried and left floating somewhere unknown. It may take a long time before an underlying reality of a secure feeling of belonging is restored.

The key response to eventually gaining sufficient healing from this damaging effect is the same as for general anxiety—endurance. One must simply close one's mind to all disturbing thoughts and feelings. Never try to analyze them; this is a waste of time and only strengthens them. They are simply to be ignored, no matter how difficult this may be. One must trust completely in the eventual success of building the empty forms and waiting on God to fill them. Doing this is especially important when the disconnection hits you the hardest. The stance one must ruthlessly take inside oneself is to follow the command of scripture in **Ephesians 6:13:** *Having done all, stand.* Commitment to this position must be absolute, even if, and especially if, you feel that no progress is ever going to be made.

A very effective method to make progress in this area is to replace idleness during the day with time spent outdoors in mindless pursuits. In recovery mode, I developed a habit of walking on a long pier close to home. I did this solely to practice walking or, more accurately, to learn again how to walk. But the real benefit became clear to me over several months of doing this. Engaging in mindless but easy physical activity greatly helped soothe my soul during the time when my mind was most vulnerable to disconnection attacks—

that is, when I wasn't with anyone or busy doing anything. However, beneficial mindless activity *must* be done outdoors. It simply doesn't work indoors, at least not for me. And it may not be enough to just sit outside staring at a sunset or trees in a park. This is probably too mindless. One's thoughts can wander down the pitfall pathways far too easily, although it is still much better than sitting inside. As I begin practicing walking, I like to develop a mental image of walking outside in the cool of the evening, just as Adam did with the Lord before the fall.

RECAP

A summary of the key responses that are able to bring a stroke victim back into a functioning, hopefully regained, existence is helpful as a quick reference guide. If commercial airline pilots never outgrow the need for a preflight checklist, we would certainly do well in life to emulate this tool and keep a response checklist handy. We must all remember the axioms presented earlier concerning never trusting in ourselves to get the job done or, for that matter, even remembering how we are supposed to get the job done. A pilot knows with certainty, when the checklist is completed, that the flight is good to go. Using a recap guide accomplishes two things.

First is it forces us to identify what is going on with us at a specific time of stress or discomfort. We must ask ourselves, "What is exactly going on with me right now? Am I just weary? Am I under anxiety? Did I just get hit with a disconnection attack? Am I resenting being around people again? Did I just get jealous of those joggers at the park? Am I just irritated because I can't seem to drive very well right now? Is it a combination of things making me feel hopeless again? Or, God forbid, am I just being immature and falling into self-pity or foolishly lashing out at people from frustration?" Reading down a list of the symptoms of a stroke can be amazingly effective to isolate your current problem.

Second, it shows us clearly, or rather reminds us clearly, what is the correct key response to what ails us at any given time. Move down the list, stop at the symptom that seems best to describe how you are feeling, go across to the next column, read what you are supposed to do, and finally, do what it says. Don't think about it, and for the love of God, certainly, don't analyze it—just do what it says.

Why is a simple list so important? One global reason is that it is impossible to manage anything until it has been measured. If a person never keeps track of income and expense, it is *impossible* to develop a budget and manage monthly finances. If a stroke victim never practices identifying what is going on internally, it is *impossible* to manage debilitating effects. I remember clearly that I didn't get serious about managing my finances until after I bought my first house. I had been accustomed to the luxury of always easily living within my means, but those days were quickly over. I soon had to measure everything and was then able to begin managing my money. Before having a stroke, one enjoyed the luxury of seldom being overwhelmed or even significantly uncomfortable in life. After a stroke, those days are immediately over, and the time to engage in measurement and management have inescapably descended upon you.

The following is a list to refer to at times of discomfort or stress to help give clarity to what is going on and what to do about it.

Symptom or Effect	**Key Responses**
Heavy Anxiety	a. Take medication and complete rest.
	b. Engage with family or friends.
Moderate Anxiety	a. Stay busy with simple tasks.
	b. Ignore and endure.
Heavy Weariness	a. Get completely alone and completely rest.
Moderate Weariness	a. Perform therapy exercises.
	b. Do *not* engage with family or friends.
Heavy Emptiness	a. Get out of doors and do mindless activity.
	b. Engage with others, *not* family or friends.
Moderate Emptiness	a. Stay busy with simple tasks.
	b. Ignore and endure.
	c. Get out of doors.

Heavy Desire for Isolation	a. Get alone and perform devotions.
	b. Go to a hospital and wander around.
Moderate Desire for Isolation	a. Force yourself to visit or call somebody.
	b. Go to a public place and walk around.
	c. Do not go out of doors.
Heavy Disconnection	a. Pretend you have a solid steel garage door on the back of your head. Slam it down. Keep your mind as empty as possible and endure.
	b. Stand and endure.
Moderate Disconnection	a. Meditate on your latest "California plan."
	b. Read science-fiction books.
	c. Stand and endure.
Heavy Anger	a. Get alone *as soon as possible.*
	b. If you are driving, *pull over immediately.*
	c. Instead of getting mad at God, tell him how mad you are, that counts as a prayer, and he will help. If you still get mad at God, tell him that too. He already knows, anyway, and that still counts as a prayer, and he will still help.

Moderate Anger

a. Exercise self-control. Pretend it's a therapy exercise because that's exactly what it is.
b. If you are driving, pull into a convenience store, buy a snack, and call up someone who you are not mad at and talk about anything but anger.
c. If you are at home, attack a task that you have not been able to get done and keep going until it's done.

FINAL THOUGHT

There may be a significant number of stroke victims who do not appear to have a problem with anger, other than just the initial evidence of frustration with performing tasks. It could be possible that none of the discussion presented previously concerning blaming oneself or God applies to these individuals. If this is the case, one of two things has occurred. The stroke victim must be an exceptional human being with an enviable personality and disposition, what most of us refer to as "saints." Would that we all could claim a membership in that number.

However, for those more average individuals, such as myself, there is another disturbing section in scripture toward which a stroke victim may gravitate. This is found in **Ecclesiastes 4:1–3:** *I saw the tears of the oppressed, with no one to comfort them. The oppressors have great power, and their victims are helpless. So I concluded that the dead are better off than the living. But most fortunate of all are those who are not yet born. For they have not seen all the evil that is done under the sun.*

A close friend of mine who had a stroke about ten years ago eventually went down this path—that is, my friend simply gave up completely. This is the position that it is, best of all, never to have been born into this world. I'm glad to say that after several years spent in this self-sentence of oblivion; he has begun to take steps of engaging the world again. It is noteworthy that before sinking into this position, although handicapped physically, he was moving around independently. But after just a few months of complete inactivity, he could no longer move without a walker. Again, we are intricately connected in body and soul. The state of one affects the other. Degeneration in the soul adversely affects the body and vice versa.

Although I felt the oblivion magnet pulling on me at some crucial times, I never embraced it. I wish it was because of "saint" status, but I'm afraid it was just much easier for me to use my abundant anger to energize my ornery German soul and just keep plowing. Consequently, I have nothing to say as to how to pull oneself up out of the slimy oblivion pit. But I suspect that extreme miserableness finally holds sway and recovery steps are finally began. Or perhaps shame fills a person in this state when confronted by an exceptional loved one, who finally figures out what is going on.

The reason for bringing up this final topic is to simply point out that friends and family may not have the faintest idea that the victim has been dwelling on the oblivion path for a long time. I learned very quickly not to disagree with family about their "full recovery" position, even before my ten days in the hospital were over. I just kept my thoughts to myself and kept the peace and let them think what they wanted to think. A stroke victim can easily give sufficient feedback to show convincingly that he or she is still "fighting the good fight" when, in fact, they have thrown in the proverbial towel months and months ago. They know that it is nearly impossible for anyone to understand what it is like in their world, so there is zero reason to bother sharing. Perhaps this is the saddest situation that may occur from a stroke.

www.ingramcontent.com/pod-product-compliance
Lightning Source LLC
LaVergne TN
LVHW061558070526
838199LV00077B/7095